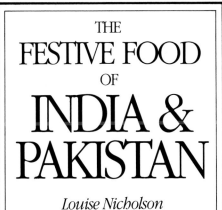

THE
FESTIVE FOOD
OF
INDIA &
PAKISTAN

Louise Nicholson

ILLUSTRATED BY SALLY MALTBY

KYLE CATHIE LIMITED

To Oliver

First published 1992 by
Kyle Cathie Limited
3 Vincent Square London SW1P 2LX

Copyright © 1992 by Louise Nicholson
Illustrations copyright © 1992 by Sally Maltby

ISBN 1 85626 051 8

A CIP catalogue record for this book is available from the British Library

Designed by Geoff Hayes

Acknowledgements
The author would like to thank Javed Abdulla, Mallika Akbar, Rati
Chandaria, Manjit Gill, Yasmin Hosain, Begum Husain, M.M. Kaye, Aruna
Pasricha and Manju Shah, and the Suruchi Restaurant for their generous
advice and contributions.

Notes:

Food suppliers: Though most of the spices and herbs in these recipes
are now readily available in the West, the following stores will send
goods: Taj Store in Brick Lane and Ali Bros at 43 Fashion Street, both
East End, have been recommended.
Spices: The fresher a spice is, the better. If fresh is unavailable, buy
whole spices and grind as required. Adjust the specified quantities to
suit personal taste. The masalas can be made in larger quantities than
needed, then stored in an airtight jar. To keep fresh ginger, chilli and
garlic on tap, buy them in quantity, peel or deseed, then grind each to
a paste, freeze in ice-cube trays and store in plastic bags in the freezer.
One cube thaws to about a tablespoonful but can be used straight
from the freezer.
Rices and pulses: These should be washed 3 or 4 times, until the
water runs clear. If the recipe demands soaking, this is to soften and
will help cooking.
Servings: Each recipe serves 6 people. An Indian meal comprises
several dishes, the number depending upon how many are to be fed,
the importance of the occasion and how much time the cook has.

Contents

Republic Day

January 26 is a national holiday – and one of the few fixed dates in the festival calendar. It marks the day in 1950 when the newly created independent Republic of India was inaugurated and its Constitution came into force. The place to be is the capital, New Delhi, where Sir Edwin Lutyens' city is the backdrop for a spectacular day-long parade.

Crowds from all over India gather in the chilly morning all along Raj Path, the three-mile-long processional route. The President leads the parade in his ceremonial coach, escorted by the President's Body Guard founded by Warren Hastings in 1773. Then follow giant thematic floats representing each state and decorated with flowers, images of gods, and tableaux of locals singing and dancing. Between them come legions of folk dancers and literally hundreds of gaily caparisoned elephants and camels, while above flies a helicopter in full elephant fancy-dress showering rose-petals. Meanwhile the folk-dance festival fills the cultural halls each evening, the government buildings twinkle with miles of fairy lights, and pavement stall-holders do a roaring trade.

Chaat

Street snacks are a vital part of Indian life and chaat stalls are found throughout India. The spicy mixture has infinite local varieties but usually includes something fried, some curd, chutney and garnishes, and it is always eaten cold. The renowned Delhi chaats tend to include dry mango and fresh mint and be savoury or fruit based.

Dahi Bhalla Chaat

The masala:
30g/1oz each of cumin seed and black peppercorns
2teaspoons black cardamom seeds
1teaspoon green cardamom seeds
2.5cm/1inch stick of cinnamon
3teaspoons yellow chilli powder
2teaspoons black salt powder

In a frying-pan, quickly dry roast all ingredients
except the chilli and salt powder. Blend or pound
all to a fine powder, combine with the chilli and salt
and set aside.

The saunth (sweet mango chutney):
3teaspoons cumin seeds
1teaspoon each of black salt,
    black peppercorns and
    black cardamom seeds
50g/2oz mango powder
250ml/⅓pint/1cup water
250g/8½oz/1cup sugar

In a frying-pan, dry roast
the cumin seeds, then
blend or pound finely
with the salt,
peppercorns and
cardamom seeds. Sieve
the mango powder and
heat in the water,
whisking continuously
until it thickens to a
sauce-like consistency.
Add the sugar and spices
and cook gently for 5
minutes. Sieve.

11

The bhallas:
300g/10½oz urad dhal (white split gram bean)
   without husk
a pinch of asafetida
oil for deep frying

1 Soak the urad dhal for 1 hour. Drain and blend to
a fine, fluffy paste (do not add water or it will be too
thin). Dissolve the asafetida in a teaspoon of water
and add to the paste.
2 In a deep, heavy saucepan, heat some oil to a
moderate heat. With wet hands, shape the paste into
small balls and carefully drop into the hot oil. Fry
until crisp and golden brown. (You can add raisins
and nuts before frying, in which case the finished
chaat will be called Dahi Gujia.)

To assemble the Dahi Bhalla Chaat:
You need, in addition to the masala, saunth and
bhallas:

500ml/16fl oz/2cups yoghurt

1 Soak the bhallas in lukewarm water for 30 minutes
and then drain and squeeze off moisture.
2 Whisk the yoghurt with a little salt.
3 Arrange the bhallas on a plate and sprinkle with
chilli powder and chaat masala. Mask with the
yoghurt, pour some saunth over and sprinkle a little
extra chilli powder for decoration.

Aloo Podina Chaat

1teaspoon each of cumin seeds, coriander seeds and
  salt
6 medium-sized potatoes, boiled in their jackets,
  peeled and cubed
2 small cucumbers, peeled, seeded and cubed
2teaspoons lemon juice
¼teaspoon each of black and red pepper
115g/4oz chopped fresh mint leaves

1 In a frying-pan, quickly dry roast the cumin and
coriander seeds, and then blend until fine.
2 Mix the diced potato and cucumber, tossing in the
salt and lemon juice. Add the spices and mint,
mixing gently to prevent the potato breaking up.

Id Ul-Fitr

This Muslim festival celebrates the end of Ramadan, the ninth month of the Muslim calendar which, since it is lunar, falls at a different time each year. It was during Ramadan that the Prophet Muhammed received his revelation. To commemorate it, the faithful over the age of twelve do not eat or drink during daylight hours for the whole month, thirty days. As the Qur'an decrees, they must 'strictly observe the fast from dawn until nightfall' and 'be at their devotions in the mosque'.

The moment the sun sets in the Islamic communities of the North-west Frontier Province of Pakistan there is a mad rush to the cafés for *iftari* (breakfast) which may include sizzling kebabs and large bowlfuls of haleem (grains cooked with meat, page 60) with large parathas and washed down with hot, sweet tea. But the feasting at the end of Ramadan surpasses all and may include roasting a whole goat or lamb stuffed with spices and rice. The raan of lamb, easier to fit into a Western oven, is equally popular.

Raan of Lamb

While this and its pulao are cooking in the distinctive North-west Frontier masala, the aroma of spices will be almost intoxicatingly mouth-watering.

1.35–1.8kg/3–4lb leg of lamb
1tablespoon/1½tablespoons corn oil or clarified
   butter

The garam masala:
5cm/2inch piece of cinnamon
20 black peppercorns
8 large black cardamom pods
12 cloves
1teaspoon black cumin seeds

The marinade paste:
2 medium heads of garlic (about 20 cloves), skinned
  and ground
2.5cm/1inch piece of fresh ginger, peeled and
  ground
½teaspoon red cayenne pepper
1teaspoon each of ground cinnamon, white cumin
  and salt
2teaspoons yoghurt

1 To make the masala, coarsely grind all ingredients.
2 To make the marinade paste, mix all ingredients
well.
3 Cut any surplus fat from the lamb, and make deep
slits all over the meat. Rub in the paste, pushing it
deep into the cuts to allow the flavour to penetrate
the meat. Rub over the oil, cover and leave for
several hours or overnight; the longer the better.
4 Before cooking, scoop up the paste and rub into
the meat again, then sprinkle over 1teaspoon of the
garam masala.
5 Seal for 20 minutes in a preheated 230°C/450°F/
gas8 oven, until brown, then turn down the oven to
190°C/375°F/gas5 for 1½ hours, until it is very well
done, turning over once.
6 Remove from the oven, sprinkle with 1 more
teaspoon of garam masala to give a fresh aroma, rest
it for 15 minutes, then carve.

Pulao

2 medium-sized onions
1tablespoon/1½tablespoons vegetable oil

The yakhni (meat soup):
1tablespoon/1½tablespoons vegetable oil
675g/1½lb shoulder of lamb, cut into 2.5cm/1inch
  pieces
6 large garlic cloves, peeled and crushed
2 tomatoes, chopped
1teaspoon salt

900g/2lb/4cups Basmati rice
2teaspoons salt
1teaspoon vegetable oil
garam masala (prepared for the raan of lamb)
½teaspoon ground black cumin

1 Slice the onions finely and pat dry. In a frying-pan,
heat the oil and fry the onions on a high heat until
deep brown – this caramelizing gives the pulao its
distinctive colour. Drain on kitchen paper, then
pound to a paste.
2 To make the yakhni, heat the oil in a saucepan
and fry the meat for 2 minutes. Add the garlic and
tomatoes. Stir until the meat is golden brown. Add
the salt and stir until the tomatoes are cooked,
splashing with a little water to prevent sticking. Add
the onion paste and 575ml/1pint/2½cups water,
cover and cook on a medium heat until the meat is
tender, about 1½ hours. Then raise the heat to
reduce the liquid by about a half.
3 Wash the rice and soak it for 10 minutes. In a large
saucepan, bring 2.25litres/4pints/10½cups water to
a furious boil. Add the rice and salt and boil for 5
minutes, cooking only until the rice grains are soft at
their ends but still hard in the centre. Drain.

4 To assemble, take a large, ovenproof, heavy-bottomed pan and pour in a teaspoon of oil. Using a slotted spoon, lay half the rice on the bottom, then all the meat on top of it. Sprinkle with ½teaspoon of garam masala and 100ml/4fl oz/½cup yakhni liquid round the sides so it seeps down to give the traditional brown-and-white, two-colour effect. Sprinkle over another ½teaspoon of garam masala and the cumin. The pulao should come halfway up the pan.

5 Cover with a tight layer of foil and the lid. Cook on a high heat for 2 minutes, then continue cooking in a preheated 150°C/300°F/gas2 oven for 45 minutes. Before serving, give the pan a good shake.

Pongal

This is the January rice harvest festival of South India, celebrated in particular in Tamil Nadu. Four days of holiday celebrations begin with Bhogi, when spring cleaning and bonfires of old possessions drive evil spirits out of the houses. The women draw exquisite *kolams* (rice paste patterns) on the great rice pot, the stove and the doorstep.

The next day is Pongal itself. Families bath and massage each other and put on new clothes. They then feast on newly harvested rice boiled up with sugar-cane, turmeric and other ingredients in the decorated pot. When the froth is *pongu* – boiling over – some is offered to Surya, the sun god, and the more it boils over the better the year ahead will be. The next day is Maattu (cattle) Pongal, when the cows and bullocks are lovingly washed, sprinkled with turmeric to ward off evil, anointed with red powder, garlanded and their horns painted bright colours. Then they have their dish of Pongal rice before being paraded round the streets.

Thali

Thali simply means platter. *Katori* (little pots) containing different dishes are arranged round the edge of the thali in a specific order to balance the flavours. They are eaten with the fingers or teaspoons from left to right, beginning with a pulse, progressing through vegetables to yoghurt, then possibly something fried and finally the sweet dish. The steaming boiled rice piled in the centre can be supplemented with breads such as fried puri. The number of *katoris* varies from the basic four – a pulse, vegetable, yoghurt and sweet – right up to thirty for a special marriage feast. The following recipes are all for a southern thali.

18

Sambar of Arhar Dhal
(SPLIT RED GRAM)

225g/8oz/1cup split red gram
½teaspoon each of turmeric and salt
a piece of tamarind the size of a lemon

The sambar masala:
scant tablespoon/1tablespoon mustard seeds
1 onion, finely chopped
a pinch of fenugreek seeds
1 small cinnamon stick
3tablespoons/4tablespoons clarified butter
scant tablespoon/1tablespoon small yellow split
   peas
2teaspoons coriander seeds
2 whole red chillies, broken
2tablespoons grated coconut flesh
6 curry leaves
A mixture of vegetables such as onions, potatoes,
   katu (white pumpkin), marrow, etc, cut into large
   pieces

1 Cook the gram in water with the turmeric and salt,
mash and set aside.
2 Extract the tamarind juice by soaking the tamarind
in 100ml/4fl oz/½cup hot water for 3 minutes, then
squeezing the juice into the water.
3 To make the sambar masala, fry the mustard
seeds, onion, fenugreek seeds and cinnamon in the
clarified butter for 2 minutes, add the split peas and
fry for 2 minutes. Add the coriander seeds, chillies
and coconut and fry for 1 further minute. Finally,
add the curry leaves.
4 Add the vegetables and cook, stirring, for
3 minutes. Add the tamarind water and cook until
the vegetables are soft. Stir in the mashed gram.

Tari Aloo
(FRAGRANT POTATOES)

900g/2lb potatoes

The masala:
75ml/4tablespoons/½cup vegetable oil
1½teaspoons black mustard seeds
3tablespoons/¼cup fresh ginger, peeled and finely chopped
2 green chillies, seeded and finely sliced
1½tablespoons/2tablespoons ground coriander
1½teaspoons ground turmeric
1teaspoon paprika
675g/1½lb onions, skinned and chopped
3teaspoons salt
2teaspoons lemon or lime juice
4tablespoons/½cup chopped fresh coriander leaves

1 Boil the potatoes in their jackets, drain and put in cold water. Peel and cut into large chunks.
2 To make the masala, heat the oil in a heavy-bottomed pan and add the mustard seeds. When they splutter, add the ginger and chillies and fry for 2 minutes. Add the coriander, turmeric and paprika and stir.
3 Add the potato chunks and onions and fry, stirring frequently, for 10 minutes. Add the salt and 32fl oz/1⅔pints/4cups of hot water, cover and simmer for a further 10 minutes. Mash one or two pieces of potato to thicken the sauce, then sprinkle with lemon or lime juice and the fresh coriander.

Note: This is delicious served with a herb raita.

Tamarind Rice

Although plain boiled rice is quite adequate, this special rice is more celebratory.

500g/1lb 2oz/2¼cups rice
175ml/6fl oz/¾cup coconut or sunflower oil
5 red chillies
1teaspoon each of black mustard seeds, turmeric, fenugreek seeds
a pinch of asafetida
100ml/4fl oz/½cup tamarind juice, prepared as for Sambar (see page 19)
1tablespoon/1½tablespoons each of coriander seeds, sesame seeds, cashew nuts, peanuts and cooked chick-peas
a few curry leaves
1tablespoon/1½tablespoons coconut or sunflower oil

1 Boil the rice until it is three-quarters cooked. Drain and spread over a plate. Sprinkle over half of the oil and leave to cool.
2 Heat the rest of the oil in a frying-pan. Add the chillies, mustard seeds, turmeric, fenugreek seeds and asafetida. Then add the tamarind juice and a pinch of salt, and cook until thick. Cool.
3 Dry roast and grind the coriander and sesame seeds, then sprinkle over the rice.
4 Fry the cashews, peanuts and chick-peas for a few minutes and mix into the rice.
5 Fry the curry leaves and add to the rice along with the spice mixture and the remaining tablespoon of (hot) oil. Mix well, cover and place in a preheated 190°C/375°F/gas5 oven for 30 minutes.

Horse and Cattle Fair

In late February the biggest and best horses, cattle, sheep, buffaloes, bulls and camels from each district of Pakistan arrive in Lahore with their keepers to attend the annual Horse and Cattle Fair. It is held in the great Fortress Stadium, just inside the Cantonment, and aims to encourage good breeding. Proud owners parade their animals round the pavilion in front of a panel of judges who award prizes of gleaming trophies and cups every day. There are stalls for equipment, trinkets and food – including Lahore's famous kebabs – and a full programme of entertainment including the unlikely feat of a camel dance.

Just as beautiful as the animals are their proud owners who all wear their local dress. The tall, black-bearded and fearsome Pathans from the North-west Frontier come dressed in their woollen hats and beige shawls. The Baluchis wear light colours and big white turbans, whereas the farmers from Sindh keep to their khaki tones and brighten the crowd with their bright green, red, blue and white turbans. The Punjabi farmers are the most numerous, for Lahore is the capital of the agriculturally rich Punjab. They wear a brightly bordered *dehband* – cloth which is wound round and then left to trail the ground – and exotic golden pointed shoes.

Lahore Kebabs and Chops

The bazaars of Lahore are famous for their foodstalls of kebabs, chops and parathas and for their cafés clustered outside the old Mughal gates.

The marinade:
50ml/3tablespoons/¼cup yoghurt
½teaspoon each of ground coriander and black cumin
¼teaspoon cayenne pepper
1teaspoon each of salt and garam masala (see Raan of Lamb, page 14)

800g/1¾lb lamb cut into small cubes, or 6 small lamb chops
2tablespoons/3tablespoons oil

1 onion, sliced
1 seeded green chilli, sliced
garam masala (see page 15)
3 tablespoons/¼cup chopped fresh coriander
lemon wedges

1 Mix together the marinade ingredients and marinate the meat for at least 1 hour.
2 For kebabs, thread the meat on to skewers, brush with oil, and cook over glowing charcoals or beneath a hot grill, turning frequently. Serve immediately with onion rings and green chillies.
3 For chops, brush with oil and cook as above. Serve sprinkled with garam masala and decorated with onion rings, chopped coriander and lemon wedges.

Fresh Mint Chutney

This is quick to prepare and goes well with all grilled meats. The quantity of each ingredient will depend on taste.

8tablespoons/1cup mint leaves
2 green chillies, seeded
¼teaspoon each of salt and sugar
2tablespoons/3tablespoons yoghurt
1teaspoon fresh lime juice (if unavailable use fresh lemon juice)

Blend or grind the mint leaves, chillies, salt and sugar. Gradually stir in the yoghurt and lime juice.

Paratha

Although most Indian breads are difficult to make, these are easy. They are eaten bigger and thicker in Lahore than further down in the sub-continent.

115g/4oz/1cup each of brown and white wheat flour
½teaspoon salt
1teaspoon oil
250ml/8floz/1cup water

1 Mix the flours and salt in a bowl and make a well. Add the oil and half of the water. Using one hand, gradually mix to a hard dough, adding a little more water as needed.
2 Roll out a piece of the dough the size of a tangerine to make a circle of 15–18cm/6–7inches diameter. Cook in a hot, dry frying-pan, adding a teaspoon of oil as it cooks on each side. Turn until rosy brown on both sides. Repeat until you have as many paratha as you need.

Holi

The arrival of spring and the beginning of a new year is celebrated across Northern India on full moon at the end of February or beginning of March. For pure enjoyment and colour, it is best seen in Rajasthan.

In the days running up to Holi, housewives do their spring cleaning. On Holi eve, each community builds a great bonfire of sticks and unwanted possessions, decorating the base with coloured powder patterns. At sunset, the bonfires are lit to symbolize the end of one year and a fresh start for the next. Householders singe a bunch of fresh green lentils in the purifying flames, then eat them ceremoniously at home as the all-night celebrations begin.

On Holi itself, laws and social conventions are suspended from dawn to noon. Men and women flirt, playing holi by squirting pink water at one another or throwing clouds of pink, mauve, green and saffron powder. The men sing and dance through the streets, banging the Holi rhythm out on a *chang*, a huge tambourine-shaped drum. In Jaisalmer, the walled desert city where tradition is strong, the women watch from upstairs balconies as the former Maharaja continues his ancient duty and sits enthroned in the street to receive token gifts from his people – who later receive similar tokens in return.

Khuda Khargosh
(STUFFED RABBIT)

The traditionally fearsome Rajasthani warriors enjoy game of all kinds, from rabbit and partridge to grouse, snipe and quail.

900g–1.35kg/2–3lb rabbit, skinned and dressed

The marinade:
1 onion, finely sliced
100ml/4fl oz/½cup clarified butter
12 each of cardamom pods and cloves
10cm/4inch stick of cinnamon
¾teaspoon each of ground mace and nutmeg
2teaspoons hot chilli powder
1½tablespoons/2tablespoons ground coriander
½teaspoon saffron, heated and crumbled
110g/4oz/½cup dried apricots or figs, finely
   chopped
scant tablespoon/1tablespoon crushed garlic

The stuffing:
115g/4oz/½cup rice
1teaspoon salt
1tablespoon/1½tablespoons oil
450g/1lb minced lamb
1 onion, finely chopped
scant tablespoon/1tablespoon fresh green chilli,
   seeded and ground
2tablespoons/3tablespoons fresh ginger, peeled and
   ground
110g/4oz/½cup seedless raisins
75g/2½oz/½cup chopped almonds

1 For the marinade, fry the onion in the butter until dark brown and caramelized; drain on kitchen paper and pound to a paste. Blend or pound the cardamom, cloves, cinnamon, mace and nutmeg to a fine powder, then add the onions for a few seconds. Add the remaining ingredients and blend until smooth. Prick the rabbit all over and rub in the marinade, inside and out. Leave for at least 4 hours, or preferably overnight.

2 For the stuffing, boil up 150ml/5fl oz/¾cup water, add the rice and salt and boil uncovered for 5 minutes. Cover and remove from the heat (the rice will continue to cook in its steam). In a frying-pan, heat the oil and brown the mince. Remove from the heat, add the half-cooked rice and all other ingredients and mix.

3 Stuff and truss the rabbit, and wrap in a double layer of silver foil, crimping the edges and leaving the head open. Roast in a preheated 230°C/450°F/gas8 oven for 30 minutes, then turn down the heat to 190°C/375°F/gas5 and roast for a further 90 minutes, keeping the meat propped on the pan side or on an upturned ramekin to prevent the juices running out. Serve whole or in pieces.

Kitchera
(RICE AND LENTILS)

Millet, wheat and other grains that grow well in the dry Thar Desert are a staple part of the Rajasthan diet. The Mughal emperor Jehangir particularly liked this kitchera, and ate it on his meatless days.

225g/8oz/1cup rice
225g/8oz/1cup moong dhal (yellow split mung beans)
150ml/5fl oz/¾cup clarified butter
2 medium onions, finely sliced
3teaspoons salt
a pinch of ground cloves
½teaspoon ground cardamom
1teaspoon ground cumin
250ml/8fl oz/1cup milk
250ml/8fl oz/1cup cream
a knob of butter

1 Wash the rice and beans together, then soak for 2 hours.
2 In a heavy-bottomed, ovenproof casserole, heat a little of the butter and fry the onion until golden brown, remove with a slotted spoon and drain.
3 Drain the rice and beans. Add the salt, cloves, cardamom and cumin. Fry in the remaining butter in the casserole for 10 minutes, stirring constantly so the rice absorbs the butter and turns golden brown. Add 500ml/16fl oz/2cups hot water and boil uncovered until it is absorbed, stirring with a fork occasionally.
4 Heat the milk and cream and add to the rice mixture. Bring to the boil, cover and cook in a preheated 190°C/375°F/gas5 oven for 20 minutes. Before serving, add a knob of butter and, with the lid on, give the pot a good shake.

Gangaur

About two weeks after Holi, this March festival is celebrated with greatest devotion in the lake-filled Rajasthan city of Udaipur. The long festival celebrates the goddess Gauri, better known as Parvati. She is the wife of Shiva, one of the Hindu Trinity, and is goddess of abundance, fertility and marital bliss. Her name also means yellow, the colour of ripened wheat.

For eighteen days devout women dress in fine clothes and carry water-filled bronze or brass vessels on their heads to the Gauri-Parvati temple, singing mystical songs as they go and then anointing the flower-bedecked goddess. During this period, they pray for marital bliss and faithfulness, set up painted wooden images of Gauri in their homes and eat only vegetarian food. On the final day, the ladies wear saffron yellow clothes and process, singing all the way, to take the Gauri image from her temple to a ceremonial bath in Lake Pichola, and the image of Shiva is brought to collect his bride in a pageant of caparisoned horses and elephants.

Soweeta
(LAMB WITH WHEAT)

While the orthodox keep to vegetarian food, plenty of families descended from the warrior Rajputs of Mewar enjoy this robust meat dish.

The masala:
1½tablespoons/2tablespoons fresh ginger, peeled
  and ground
scant tablespoon/1tablespoon ground coriander
2teaspoons salt

6 whole dried red chillies
5 onions, thinly sliced
75ml/3fl oz/½cup clarified butter
675g/1½lb lean lamb, cut into 5cm/2inch cubes
250ml/8fl oz/1cup yoghurt, beaten smooth
285g/10oz/2cups whole wheat grains
700ml/1¼pint/3cups full cream milk, heated
½teaspoon salt
50ml/2fl oz/¼cup clarified butter

1 To make the masala, finely blend all the
ingredients.
2 Seed the chillies, then soak in a cup of hot water.
3 In a heavy-bottomed, ovenproof casserole, fry 1 of
the onions in the butter until golden. Add the meat
and masala, and fry for 5 minutes. Add 500ml/16fl
oz/2cups water and boil gently, uncovered, until the
liquid is absorbed. Stir in the yoghurt and the
remaining sliced onion, and continue cooking until
the yoghurt is absorbed.
4 Meanwhile, wash the wheat and boil uncovered in
700ml/1¼pints/3cups salted water until all the water
is absorbed. Stir the wheat into the meat, pour over
the heated milk, and bring to the boil. Cover tightly
with foil and the saucepan lid and cook in a
preheated 190°C/375°F/gas5 oven for 30 minutes,
by which time all the liquid should be absorbed.
5 Drain the red chillies and add the salt. Sauté in the
butter for 5 minutes. Serve one with each portion of
meat.

Bhindi
(OKRA)

This also works well with cauliflower florets or potatoes.

450g/1lb okra
vegetable oil
2teaspoon ground cumin seeds
½teaspoon each of red chilli powder and ground
   black pepper

1 Wash, dry and chop the okra into 2cm/½inch slices.
2 In a large, heavy-bottomed saucepan, heat 6–7cm/2–3inches of oil until a haze forms on top. Slide in the okra and fry until golden brown, remove with a slotted spoon and toss in the spices. Serve at once.

Lapsi
(WHEAT PUDDING)

Since wheat is more readily available than rice in Rajasthan, this is the favourite celebratory dessert.

700ml/25fl oz/3cups clarified butter
450g/1lb cracked wheat
1.6litres/2¾pints/7cups milk, very hot
a good pinch of saffron threads, diluted in
    50ml/2fl oz/¼cup hot water
170g/6oz/¾cup sugar
110g/4oz/½cup seedless raisins
75g/2½oz/½cup each of slivered almonds and
    slivered pistachios

1 In a heavy-bottomed, ovenproof casserole, heat the butter (reserving 75ml/3fl oz), stir in the wheat and keep stirring until it is toast-brown.
2 Pour in about two-thirds of the almost boiling milk, stir well, cover and cook on a medium heat until almost all the liquid is absorbed.
3 Add the saffron and its soaking water, the remaining butter and milk, the sugar, the raisins and half the nuts. Mix well, bring to the boil, cover tightly with foil and lid and bake in a preheated 190°C/375°F/gas5 oven for 25 minutes, by which time all the liquid should be absorbed. Garnish with the remaining nuts.

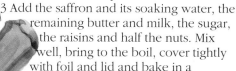

Navroze and Baisakhi

Springtime Kashmir enjoys a double celebration. The Muslims, who form the vast majority, celebrate the Shia festival of Navroze on the spring equinox, March 20. The only major Muslim festival not to follow the lunar calendar, it marks the New Year in the Old Persian calendar; on this day, by tradition, the Prophet conferred the caliphate on his son-in-law, Ali. It is a time for family feasting. In Kashmir, this means ordering the great *wazwan* (royal feast) of up to seventeen courses, which is prepared by catering firms and brought to the house.

Meanwhile, Hindus throughout northern India celebrate the spring festival of Baisakhi. In Kashmir this focuses on the spectacular blossoms for which Srinagar and the surrounding countryside are famous. Fields glow with the purples and yellows of thousands of crocus flowers from which pollen is collected to make the prized saffron that perfumes and colours celebratory food. Orchards are a dreamy mass of pale pink almond, walnut, apricot, apple and pear blossoms whose nuts and fruits are an essential ingredient of the light, subtle Kashmiri dishes as well as the rich royal Mughal cuisine. On Baisakhi, both Hindu and Muslim Kashmirs throng Srinagar's lakeside terraced gardens built by the Mughal emperors, where there is dancing in the pavilions and nightly illuminations.

Dhaniyawal Korma
(CORIANDER KORMA)

This is a favourite *wazwan* dish for Navroze. The fresh coriander is essential to its success.

1.35kg/3lb lamb, cubed
4 onions, finely chopped
500ml/16fl oz/2cups yoghurt
1teaspoon salt
½teaspoon each of ground
   cardamom and cinnamon
2teaspoons ground ginger
125ml/4½fl oz/⅔cup clarified butter
3 garlic cloves, crushed
115g/4oz/⅔cup blanched almonds
4fl oz/¼pint/½cup milk
8fl oz/⅓pint/1cup cream
8tablespoons/1cup finely chopped fresh coriander
   leaves

1 In a casserole, mix the lamb, chopped onion, yoghurt, salt, cardamom, cinnamon, ginger, clarified butter and garlic. Add water to cover. Simmer gently, half-covered, until the lamb is very tender and the liquid well reduced, almost to dryness, about 1½ hours.
2 Grind the almonds in a blender, then slowly pour in the milk. Add to the meat and mix well, then add the cream and coriander. Serve with plain rice boiled with a little saffron to make it festive.

Note: This is delicious with mint and walnut chutney, made by grinding a few walnuts and mint leaves in a blender and adding some good fresh yoghurt, a pinch of salt, black pepper and cayenne and, for extra spice, a chopped green chilli.

Aubergines with Apple

The masala:
½teaspoon each of ground fennel seeds, turmeric,
   cayenne pepper, crushed garlic and salt

100ml/6tablespoons/½cup vegetable oil
¼teaspoon asafetida
3 large, firm eating apples, cored (not peeled) and
   cut into wedges
900g/2lb aubergines, sliced crosswise

1 Combine the spices for the masala.
2 In a frying-pan, heat the oil good and hot. Add the
asafetida and the apples to lightly brown them on all
sides, then remove with a slotted spoon. Fry the
aubergines in batches, adding more oil if necessary,
until lightly browned, then drain. Return the apples,
aubergines and masala to the pan and
cook on a low heat for 10 minutes,
draining off excess oil and turning
gently so as not to break the pieces.

Kheer
(RICE PUDDING)

The nuts, saffron and kewra water lift this familiar
dish into an aromatic delight, the consistency of
which should be almost pourable.

1litre/1¾pints/4½cups full fat milk
75g/2½oz rice soaked in water for an hour, then
    drained
15g/½oz each of pistachios and skinned almonds,
    flaked
a pinch of saffron strands
1teaspoon kewra water (screwpine distilled
    essence)
250g/8½oz sugar
5–6 crushed cardamom pods
4 silver leaves

1 In a heavy-bottomed pan, slowly heat the milk,
rice, flaked pistachios and almonds, and the saffron
dissolved in the kewra water.
2 Cook very slowly, stirring regularly – the slower
the cooking, the more creamy the result. When the
milk has thickened and the rice is almost cooked,
add the sugar. When cooked, leave to cool slightly
before adding the crushed cardamom pods. Eat
warm or cool, decorated with silver leaves.

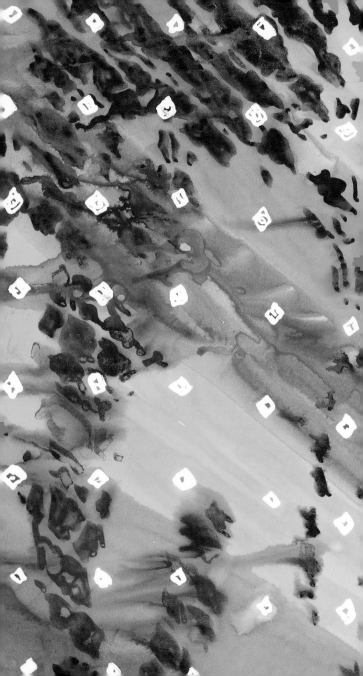

Pooram

Kerala state, bordered by the Arabian Sea and the spice-growing Nilgiri and Cardamom Hills, is distinctly different from the rest of India. And the Hindus' Pooram festival at Trichur, celebrated in April–May to honour two goddesses named Paramkavu and Thiruvambady, is like no other festival.

Although only Hindus may enter Kerala's elaborately carved wooden temples, the most spectacular parts of Pooram take place in the streets. As thousands of visitors pour in, the streets are decorated with coconut leaves, pendants and lamps, and payments are negotiated for space on rickety viewing platforms and rooftops.

On Pooram eve, thirty elephants chosen for their size and beauty of trunk, tail, ears and tusks, arrive together with their food, lorryloads of palm leaves. The next morning, they are dressed up in gold-plaited chain mail and Brahmins get up on top to hold the symbolic deity, silk parasols, whisks and peacock feather fans.

The whole party sets off on its slow, majestic, glorious day-long procession and ritual, accompanied by ear-splitting music, cheered along by the faithful who shower them with offerings of flowers and rice. After sunset, the whole procession is repeated with different music and flaming torches, ending with a massive fireworks display which lasts until dawn. Soon after, the elephants assemble for a final three hours of drumming and more fireworks.

Red Fish Curry

This hot dish, similar to some Goan fish dishes, is eaten by both the Hindu and Syrian Christian communities of Kerala. Housewives make it well in advance, and the spices both preserve it and improve it.

4 pieces of kokum (a special Kerala tamarind though ordinary tamarind will do)
1kg/2¼lb firm white fish
1tablespoon/1½tablespoons black mustard seeds
1tablespoon/1½tablespoons coconut or sunflower oil
7–8 curry leaves

The masala:
2 onions
12 garlic cloves
2.5cm/1inch piece of fresh ginger, peeled
1tablespoon/1½tablespoons chilli powder
1teaspoon turmeric
½teaspoon ground fenugreek seeds
½teaspoon black pepper

1 To make the kokum (or tamarind) water, soak the kokum in 850ml/1½pints/3¾cups water for 10 minutes, then remove it but keep the water. Then extract the juice, see page 19.

2 To make the masala, blend or grind all the ingredients together.

3 Put the fish into the reserved water from soaking the kokum. Fry the mustard seeds in the oil until they splutter. Add the masala and a little water and fry for 2 minutes. Add the curry leaves, kokum water and the kokum itself. Boil for 3–5 minutes, or more for a thicker sauce. Add the fish and bring to the boil again, then cook on a low heat for just a few minutes. Eat with brown, unhusked rice.

Payaru Thoran
(GREEN BEANS WITH COCONUT)

French beans are the closest thing to the Kerala ones, but this dish can also be made with spinach, shredded cabbage, peas or carrots, as long as they are cut small for the fast cooking.

500g/1lb 2oz finely sliced French beans
2 onions and 1 green chilli, both finely sliced
⅓teaspoon salt
1tablespoon/1½tablespoons coconut or vegetable oil
1tablespoon/1½tablespoons black mustard seeds
½coconut, grated
½teaspoon turmeric
1–2 red chillies, each broken in two

1 Combine the beans, half of the sliced onion, the chilli and salt.
2 Fry the rest of the onion and mustard seeds in the oil until the seeds splutter. Add the bean mixture, but no water. Cook on a low heat and when almost ready add the coconut, turmeric and red chillies. Cook for another 5 minutes and serve.

Kachi More
(HEATED BUTTERMILK)

This is a favourite refreshing Kerala drink, enjoyed with meals and in between. It keeps well in the fridge for several days.

The masala:
1 small onion and 1 green chilli, thinly sliced
½tablespoon black mustard seeds
1tablespoon/1½tablespoons coconut or sunflower
  oil
½teaspoon ground fenugreek seeds
¼teaspoon turmeric
7–8 curry leaves

500ml/16fl oz/2cups yoghurt
salt

1 Fry the onion, chilli and mustard seeds in the oil, keeping the heat low. Add the fenugreek, turmeric and curry leaves and cook for another minute. Do not add water unless it is sticking. Cool.

2 Beat the yoghurt smooth, thinning it with a little water. Add the spices and return to an extremely low heat for 5–6 minutes to percolate the flavour through, stirring all the time. Cool and add a little salt. Keep in the fridge.

Swarantsri Pratikraman

This festival, held in August–September, is celebrated by all Jains throughout India. Jainism emerged in the sixth century, breaking away from rigid Hinduism in search of a more contemplative and spiritual life. Its leader was Mahavira, who lived as a naked ascetic for twelve years before becoming *jina*, meaning conqueror. His followers do not believe in a god but they do believe the world is infinite and that there is reincarnation and salvation. These are found through, amongst other efforts, temple building and *ahimsa*, reverence for all life. *Ahimsa* demands strict vegetarianism which includes no roots. So, with garlic, onion, potato and ginger forbidden, Jains have developed a distinctive cuisine.

Swarantsri Pratikraman is a time for meditating and repenting quietly. A week of feasting or semi-feasting to cleanse the soul is reinforced with meditation, readings from the life of Mahavira, and morning and evening worship. On the eighth day, Jains gather at their local temple or hall for the final prayers where they ask forgiveness for all living creatures of the world and for all past bad deeds. The next day there is a celebratory meal which follows the local traditional dishes but adheres to Jain restrictions. These recipes are from a Gujarat Jain family.

Kudi

This sweet-and-sour yoghurt soup is served in a *katori* (little dish) with a teaspoon, beside the thali plate that holds vegetables, pulse, sweet, rice and a pile of puris; all best eaten with the fingers. Finish with a drink of lassi – yoghurt and water, with a dash of salt and cumin powder.

The masala:
½teaspoon each of coriander seeds, fenugreek seeds, white cumin seeds
3 each of curry leaves and cloves
a pinch of asafetida

250ml/8fl oz/1cup plain yoghurt mixed with 250ml/8fl oz/1cup water
1tablespoon/1½tablespoons gram flour
1teaspoon salt
1teaspoon clarified butter
½teaspoon each of ground fresh ginger and green chilli
½tablespoon jaggery or brown sugar
1teaspoon chopped coriander leaves

1 Combine the masala ingredients.
2 Whisk together the watered yoghurt, gram flour and salt.
3 In a large saucepan, heat the butter, add the masala, fry for a few seconds and then add the yoghurt mixture. Bring to a boil, stirring continuously to prevent curdling. Add the ground ginger and chilli and simmer very gently for 10–15 minutes – it will not curdle now and only needs stirring occasionally. Add the sugar, then the chopped coriander leaves and serve hot.

Aubergine with Fenugreek Leaves

2 aubergines
1½tablespoons/2tablespoons vegetable oil
4tablespoons/½cup chopped fresh fenugreek
    leaves, pressed down
1teaspoon each of salt and turmeric

The masala:
½teaspoon each of black mustard seeds, white
    cumin seeds and ajwain (corum seeds)
¼teaspoon asafetida

1 Cut the aubergines into chunks and put them in
water to remove any sourness.
2 In a saucepan, heat the oil, add the masala
ingredients and fry for a few seconds. Add the
chopped fenugreek, drained aubergines, salt and
turmeric. Shake the saucepan to mix. Do not cover
(or the greens turn bitter), but cook uncovered,
shaking occasionally, for 15 minutes on a low heat.
Add a little sugar if it is too sour for your taste.

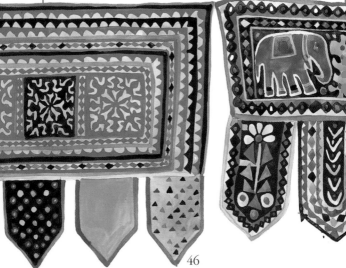

Puris

These fried, puffed-up breads are made slightly bigger for lunch than for supper.

115g/4oz/1cup brown wheat flour (wholewheat is
  too heavy)
½teaspoon salt
1½tablespoons/2tablespoons vegetable oil
100ml/4fl oz/½cup milk

1 Put the flour in a bowl, make a well and add the salt, oil and milk. Using a hand, form a firm dough, adding a little extra water or flour as needed.
2 In a small wok, heat 4cm/1½inches vegetable oil.
3 Form small balls of dough, the size of damsons, and roll out to 10cm/4inches diameter. Cook one by one, lowering each into the fat, where it puffs up immediately. Turn with a spatula, remove when golden, and build up a pile of puris on kitchen roll.

Ganpati

In Maharashtra and Orissa, the Hindu god Ganesh is celebrated at the end of September. And in Bombay festivities have turned from a private affair into a public jamboree.

In the ten-day run-up to Ganpati, every street corner and home has an image of the benign, fat-bellied god Ganesh. A human with an elephant's head, he is one of the most popular of the plethora of Hindu gods: his big belly symbolizes the universe, his trunk is bent to remove obstacles, and he is generally associated with welcome, good fortune, wisdom and prosperity.

By Ganpati, which is on full-moon day, the city is filled with more than 6000 gaudy, pink, garlanded clay images of the god, a morsel of last year's figure kneaded into this year's clay mixture. The largest and most expensive sit on great trucks and are the results of fierce competition between factory workers; the more traditional are jazzed up with flickering multi-coloured lights or electric fountains.

The faithful put on new clothes and bangles, prepare special vegetarian food including sweet modaks, and perform their worship. Then half the city parades their idols down to Chowpatty beach, carrying them on high or, for the big ones, in trucks. Amid clouds of pink powder, music and dancing, the images are finally immersed in the Arabian Sea and float into the late afternoon sun.

Steamed Modaks

These are believed to be one of the sweet-loving Ganesh's favourites and are made in every Maharashtra home at Ganpati.

The filling:
225g/8oz/1½cups coconut flesh
225g/8oz/1½cups brown sugar
a pinch of salt
1teaspoon roasted poppyseeds
½teaspoon ground cardamom

225g/8oz/2cups rice flour mixed with 575ml/1pint/
  2½cups water
1½tablespoons/2tablespoons oil
¼teaspoon salt
clarified butter to serve

1 To make the filling, mix the coconut and sugar and heat gently. Add the salt, poppyseeds and cardamom. Mix well and cook for 5 minutes.
2 In a saucepan, heat the rice flour mixture, oil and salt, stirring until it boils, then simmer for 5 minutes. Cool slightly, then knead while it is still warm.
3 Roll two small balls of dough into circles, put 1–2 tablespoons of the sweet coconut mixture on one, place the other on top and press the edges together. Repeat until all the dough and filling is used up.
4 Steam the modaks for 10 minutes and serve hot with clarified butter.

Durga Puja

This autumn festival, held in September–October, is riotously celebrated in Varanasi and Calcutta. In the first, quantities of holidays and religious observances close down schools and universities for a month. In Calcutta, the three-week-long festival stops business and is rated top of all festivals in this cosmopolitan city which prides itself on celebrating twenty official festivals varying from Christmas to Id.

Durga Puja is the general name given to the autumn Navaratra, or Nine Nights. The goddess Durga, destroyer of evil, is one of many forms of Parvati, Shiva's wife, and is portrayed as multi-limbed and riding a lion. For her festival, people consecrate a round water pot in their homes, symbolizing her auspicious presence throughout the festival.

But the big celebrations are in the streets. In Calcutta a community of craftsmen living in the city centre spends all year constructing and painting huge clay images of Durga, using straw and bamboo frames. On the first day of Navaratra, each is consecrated and becomes a temporary dwelling place for Durga. On the tenth night, marking the day Durga defeated her enemy the Bull Demon, the thousands of gaudy images are processed through the illuminated Calcutta streets, music throbbing through loud-speakers, down to the Hooghly river. There the goddess departs from her images which, now lifeless, are ceremoniously given to the river.

Dai-Sarse-Chingri
(PRAWNS WITH YOGHURT AND MUSTARD SEEDS)

Calcuttans use estuary prawns, known for their
sweetness, for this classic Bengal dish. This modern
recipe bakes rather than fries.

450g/1lb prawns
1½tablespoons/2tablespoons mustard seeds,
   preferably a mixture of yellow and black
3 green chillies, seeded
3tablespoons/4tablespoons yoghurt
1teaspoon each of turmeric and salt
1½tablespoons/2tablespoons mustard or vegetable
   oil

1 Shell the prawns, slit each back and remove the
black vein. Wash.
2 Grind or pound the mustard seeds and chillies
with 50ml/2fl oz/¼cup water.
3 Place the prawns and the mustard mixture with
the remaining ingredients in a casserole. Cover
and bake in a preheated 190°C/375°F/gas5 oven
for 1 hour. Serve
with plain rice.

Diwali

This is India's festival of lights, a Hindu festival celebrated late October–early November across the country. Clay dishes filled with oil and a wick are set on the windowsills of every home, and along the balconies, rooftops and garden walls. As the sun sets, the lamps are lit and whole villages and towns, even the capital of Delhi, twinkle throughout the evening to light the way for the gods Rama and Sita to return to their north Indian home from Lanka.

The lights also welcome Lakshmi, goddess of prosperity, wealth and pleasure, for this is also the beginning of a new Hindu financial year. In preparation, houses are spring cleaned, temples whitewashed and shops offer Diwali discounts.

On Diwali day, friends give each other boxes of sweetmeats, nuts and dried fruits, and families spend the day together gobbling them up with small fried savouries such as pakoras, and drinking plenty of tea or cool lassi. In businesses, new account books are opened and, at the auspicious hour dictated by the pandits, Lakshmi is worshipped. For entertainment, there are fairs, fireworks and gambling – he who wins on Diwali will prosper in the coming year.

Badaam Barfi
(ALMOND FUDGE)

Sweetmeats take a long time to make and are rarely made at home, but you should find this simplified recipe quite easy.

300g/11oz/2cups
   blanched almonds
500ml/16fl oz/2cups full
   cream milk
170g/6oz/¾cup sugar
55g/2oz butter
leaves of silver to decorate

1 Grease a 20cm/8inch square biscuit tray. Grind the almonds to a fine powder.
2 In a heavy-bottomed, non-stick saucepan, boil the milk on a high heat for about 10 minutes, uncovered and stirring continuously, until it is like cream soup.
3 Reduce the heat, add the sugar and cook for 2 minutes. Add the almonds and butter and cook for a further 3 minutes, stirring vigorously and scraping the fudge off the spoon with a knife.
4 Pour on to the greased tray, quickly flatten evenly and press the silver on top. While still warm, cut into rectangles or diamonds. The fudge keeps well in an airtight container.

Christmas

Although Christianity came to the sub-continent with St Thomas the Apostle's arrival in Kerala in the south, it was with the Raj wives that Christmas became a serious affair, particularly for children. The aim was to create everything just as it would be at home. As the author M. M. Kaye remembers, 'It was a point of honour to make it as Mrs Beeton as possible.'

In the run up to Christmas, every household decorated a tree, bought crackers and polished up the punch bowl. The clubs staged amateur dramatics and army garrisons gave extravagant children's parties, with conjurors, magicians, puppet shows and, to top it all, Father Christmas arriving on an elephant or camel. Piles of tiny, shining tangerines filled the bazaars, while in the kitchens fresh local spices and dried fruits went into unrivalled mince pies and Christmas puddings.

On Christmas Day, the servants gave their employers trays of fruit, sweetmeats and flowers, and received in turn money, clothes and other practical gifts. For Christmas dinner, chicken and partridge stood in for turkey and was roast plain with all the trimmings. But those on family camping trips might naughtily enjoy wild pea-hen (not the tougher peacock), which was considered sacred in many princely states and could not be eaten in town.

Christmas Punch

A pure punch contains just five ingredients – alcohol, sugar, lime juice, spice and water – since the word comes from the Hindustani meaning five. The Anglo-Indians devised their local specialities using fresh fruits and available alcohols, often exceeding the stipulated five, as this one does.

100ml/4fl oz/½cup each of fresh orange/tangerine, lime/lemon and pineapple juice
30g/1oz icing sugar
150ml/5fl oz/¾cup each of rum and Cointreau
2 bottles of claret
1 bottle of champagne
575ml/1pint/2½cups soda water

Mix the juices and sugar in the punch bowl, then add the rum, Cointreau and claret. At the moment of serving, add champagne, soda water and ice.

Snap Dragons

Like other Victorian traditions, this was played with furious excitement in Raj India right up to Independence.

Scatter a variety of nuts, sultanas and other dried fruits on a large plate. Pour over a small glass of brandy, set it alight, and take turns to snatch the nuts and fruit from the flames.

Dizzy Fruits

In M. M. Kaye's home this was a favourite which she and her sister Bets helped prepare each year.

In the late summer, put some prunes and dried apricots in a screwtop jar. Over the following months, add the bottle ends of gin, brandy, whisky, sherry and almost anything else except crème de menthe. By Christmas the fruits will have swollen and become very alcoholic, and the syrup is gloriously thick.

Prune and Claret Mould

In Anglo-India any pudding set in a mould was known affectionately as 'shape'. Despite its nursery image, the rich flavour and strong colour of this one made it a sophisticated and not too sweet dish. Jennifer Brennan, brought up in India, remembers it as a favourite with the men.

450g/1lb stoned prunes
85g/3oz sugar
½bottle of claret
1tablespoon/1½tablespoons lemon peel
5cm/2inch stick of cinnamon
1tablespoon/1½tablespoons gelatine
2tablespoons slivovitz
30 blanched almonds
250ml/8fl oz/1cup thick cream, whipped, to serve

1 Simmer the prunes, sugar, claret, lemon peel and cinnamon with 575m/1pint/2½cups water for 20–30 minutes, until the prunes have swollen.
2 Drain off the juice, discarding the lemon peel and spice. The juice should measure 300ml/½pint/ 1¼cups; reduce it by boiling if necessary. Purée the prunes.
3 Dissolve the gelatine in 3tablespoons/¼cup of the juice. Add the remaining juice and the slivovitz to the prunes and purée again, then add the gelatine juice. Put in a bowl and chill until turning firm. Stir in the almonds; and pour the mixture into a mould. To serve, turn out the mould on to a large platter and pipe swirls of cream all around the base. Serve the whole pudding chilled.

Muharram

In Islamic communities, ten days of festivities commemorate the martyrdom of Muhammed's grandson, Iman Hussain. On the sub-continent, it is best seen in Lucknow, where the Muslims follow the Shia strain of Islam and believe that the Prophet's successor is by descent through his son-in-law, Ali.

The focus is the Great Imambara. When Muharram arrives, the otherwise low-key city becomes the stage for dramatic religious demonstration. For nine days, huge *tazias* – replicas of Hussain's tomb, made of silver and brass by special craftsmen and decorated with coloured tinsel and painted panels of *mica* – are paraded by mourning men, accompanied by drummers. To increase identification with Hussain, some men lash themselves in sorrow, while others punish themselves by being suspended from a rope whose hook is pierced through the skin on their bare backs. Less harsh are the passion plays and the readings in the mosques by the *ulemas*, religious scholars. After Muharram there is family feasting on the sophisticated, smooth old court recipes for which Lucknow is famous.

Seekh Kebabs

800g/1¾lb lamb or mutton, diced
75g/2½oz lamb or mutton fat
1 green chilli, seeded and finely chopped
2tablespoon/3tablespoons fresh coriander
1½tablespoons/2tablespoons each of ginger and
　garlic, peeled and sliced
½teaspoon red chilli powder
3teaspoons poppyseeds
a pinch each of nutmeg and mace
1teaspoon garam masala (see Raan of Lamb,
　page14)
1 egg
2tablespoons/3tablespoons oil

1 Mix together the meat, the fat and all spices and mince very fine.
2 Add the egg and mix well. Refrigerate for at least 30 minutes.
3 Knead the mince on to skewers and grill over glowing charcoals or under a hot grill, turning so they are evenly brown. When almost done, brush with oil and grill for another minute.
5 Serve sprinkled with an extra dash of garam masala, thinly sliced onion rings, lemon wedges and mint chutney (see Lahore Kebabs, page 23).

Haleem

An ideal warming dish if Muharram falls in winter. One old recipe demands seven different grains; this one is more practical. But Lucknow gourmets agree that serving the haleem is always a grand ceremony, and its elaborate garnish is essential.

450g/1lb cracked wheat
140g/5oz gram dhal (split yellow peas)
1.35kg/3lb mutton on the bone, trimmed of all fat
1 small onion, chopped
500ml/16fl oz/2cups clarified butter
1½tablespoons/2tablespoons each of fresh ground
   garlic, ginger and salt

For the bouquet garni:
2 bay leaves
12 each of cloves and black peppercorns
2 5cm/2inch sticks of cinnamon
2 black cardamom pods
1teaspoon white cumin seeds

For the tempering:
1 finely chopped onion fried in 100ml/4fl oz/½cup
   clarified butter

For the garnish on the haleem:
1teaspoon garam masala (the same ingredients as
   for the bouquet garni but omit the bay leaves)
1 small onion, fried golden in clarified butter
6 fresh mint leaves

For the garnish around the haleem, one little dish each of as many of the following as possible: golden fried onions, seeded and chopped green chillies, fresh mint leaves, wedges of lemon, spring onions, plain yoghurt, garam masala

1 Wash the wheat and dhal together, then soak for 1 hour. Tie the bouquet garni ingredients in cheesecloth.

2 In a large, heavy-bottomed casserole, melt the butter and fry the onions until golden. Add the bouquet garni and the garlic, ginger and salt. Fry, stirring, for 5 minutes. Add the meat and enough water to come 10cm/4 inches higher than the mixture. Boil briskly for 5 minutes. Reduce the heat, cover and cook in a preheated 190°C/375°F/gas5 oven until the meat starts to fall off the bone, about 1½ hours.

3 Remove the bouquet garni. Give a good stir with a wooden spoon. If the occasion is special remove the meat bones.

4 Turn the haleem into a tureen. To temper it, swirl the sizzling hot fried onions over the haleem and cover immediately to trap the smoke. To serve, sprinkle with the haleem garnish. Surround with little bowls of garnishes, to which people help themselves.